Lead Magnet Theory

Limitless Lead Generation

By Zak Merezhko

This book is dedicated to those who brainstorm about their lead generation

Contents

Introduction

Welcome! This book offers a quick exploration of the world of lead magnets, presenting a range of insights and strategies rooted in research and application. This book is not intended to be an exhaustive encyclopedia; instead, it presents a concise and actionable overview of the topic, inviting both beginners and pros to explore and adapt its content to their unique business contexts. The aim is to spark ideas, inspire innovative approaches, and encourage the spirit of experimentation. As the landscape of lead magnets continues to evolve, this book serves as a point for continuous learning and adaptation. It's an invitation to engage with the material, question it, and use it as a springboard for further discovery and success in the ever-changing world of lead generation.

Please email your feedback, questions and requests to zakmerezhko@gmail.com

To connect with our lead magnet community, go to onlineleadsgroup.com

Lead Generation

The word **'lead'** has various meanings in English. In the context of this book, we focus on the business interpretation of the term, specifically referring to **'sales leads'**

For beginners, sales leads are people or entities that showed interest in your company, offer, product, service etc. They're potential clients or customers. They haven't bought yet, thus they're just a lead for now.

Before any selling begins, businesses need "prospects" or potential customers. Without reaching potential customers with compelling reasons to buy, even businesses with outstanding offerings can falter.

In ancient times, lead generation was predominantly a face-to-face endeavor. Merchants in marketplaces, craftsmen in guilds, and traders relied heavily on word-of-mouth referrals and physical presence in busy locations. Quality and reputation were paramount in these local markets. However, these methods were limited in scope and scalability.

With the advent of the printing press, the landscape of lead generation transformed. Print media enabled businesses to reach a wider audience through newspapers, posters, and billboards. The introduction of railroads and postal services further expanded these opportunities. For instance, direct mail was revolutionized by the new ability to send out comprehensive product catalogs, thus broadening the reach of businesses.

The Industrial Revolution ushered in a new era of advertising. Businesses leveraged national media, radio, and later television to reach vast audiences. The first radio advertisement in 1922 and the initial television commercial in 1941 marked significant milestones. This period also saw the rise of targeted magazine advertising and the effectiveness of direct mail campaigns.

The advent of the Internet in the late 20th century radically altered lead generation.

Online platforms offered global reach and precise targeting at a fraction of traditional costs. Search Engine Optimization (SEO), email marketing, and Pay-Per-Click (PPC) advertising became pivotal. However, this also necessitated a deeper understanding of diverse markets and more sophisticated marketing strategies.

The rise of mobile technology and social media platforms further transformed lead generation. Platforms like Facebook, founded in 2004, enabled businesses to engage with customers on a more personal level. Mobile technology meant businesses could reach consumers anytime, anywhere. Social media facilitated brand building and direct targeting, while mobile devices allowed for innovative approaches like instant call-to-action buttons and mobile-specific content.

As technology continues to evolve, so will lead generation methods. Businesses must stay abreast of trends and technologies to enhance the efficiency and effectiveness of their strategies. While tactics and tools may change, the core principle remains: understanding the target market and presenting them with compelling reasons to purchase.

Businesses continually assess their understanding of their customers and the effectiveness of their marketing strategies. Successful businesses, irrespective of the era, excel in identifying and reaching their target market with appropriate solutions.

Ask ten marketers "What's a lead and how do I generate some?" expect ten different answers back

Why is the definition not straightforward?

As mentioned earlier, a lead is typically someone who has shown interest. However, the extent and nature of this interest can vary. For some, a lead might be anyone who subscribes to a newsletter, while for others, it might be someone who has specifically requested a quote or a demo.

Different industries and business models have different ways of identifying and qualifying leads. For instance, a B2B (business-to-business) company might consider a lead as a decision-maker in a relevant company, whereas a B2C (business-to-consumer) company might view a lead as any potential customer.

Marketers employ a multitude of strategies to generate leads. The effectiveness and relevance of these strategies can differ based on the target audience, product, or market, leading to different perspectives on what constitutes a good lead.

Leads can be classified into different stages of the sales funnel, like 'MQL' (Marketing Qualified Lead) and 'SQL' (Sales Qualified Lead). Different organizations might have varying criteria for these stages, impacting how they define and pursue leads.

The tools and platforms used for lead generation can also influence definitions and strategies. For example, businesses using sophisticated CRM systems might have more detailed lead segmentation compared to those using more basic tools.

What qualifies as a lead can be subjective and based on the specific goals and experiences of a marketer or a marketing team. Personal biases and past experiences can significantly shape one's definition of a lead.

In summary, the diversity in definitions and methods for lead generation stems from the multifaceted nature of marketing itself, which is influenced by industry-specific requirements, business goals, marketing strategies, technological tools and so much more.

Why is generating leads not straightforward?

In the ever-evolving world of marketing, the concept of lead generation stands as a formidable challenge, often perceived as an intricate puzzle that marketers strive to solve. The complexity inherent in this process is not just a hurdle but also an opportunity for innovation and creativity. At the heart of lead generation lies the unpredictable and diverse terrain of consumer behavior. Each consumer's journey is a unique narrative, influenced by a myriad of factors – personal preferences, cultural influences, economic conditions, and evolving technological landscapes. This diversity means that what resonates with one individual might be irrelevant to another, presenting a substantial challenge in creating universally effective lead generation strategies. The marketing landscape is like a dynamic battlefield, where companies compete for attention in a saturated space. In this intensely competitive arena, traditional methods of lead generation often fall short. The key challenge here is not just to reach potential leads but to capture their interest compellingly and memorably. In a way that positively stimulates their brains so to speak. A common quandary in lead generation is the balance between quantity and quality. While accumulating a vast number of leads might seem advantageous, the true value lies in the quality and relevance of these leads. The pursuit of quantity can often lead to a dilution of quality, and a shift in focus is essential. But also, sometimes having a large quantity of leads at a very good price can signal an untapped niche, unrepresented consumers, or a group of people without solutions. In such cases, it might be worth reconsidering the entire business approach. This situation could represent a golden opportunity to address unmet needs or enter a less competitive market, potentially leading to significant growth and success.

Technology has revolutionized lead generation, offering tools for precision and efficiency. However, this technological boom also brings its complexities. The continuous evolution of digital platforms means that marketers must be agile, constantly learning and adapting to leverage these tools effectively.

In the face of these challenges, the concept of 'limitless' lead generation emerges not just as a theory but as a necessary evolution.

Limitless lead generation

Lead magnets, by their nature, are designed to be continually refined and enhanced. They represent a dynamic element in the marketer's toolkit, adaptable to changing market trends, consumer behaviors, and technological advancements. In this light, lead magnets are not just tools for attracting leads; they are catalysts for ongoing improvement, growth and scalability in lead generation strategies.

2008: Origin of lead magnets

In the wake of the 2008 financial crisis, the business landscape underwent a profound transformation. Companies grappled with tighter budgets and reduced consumer spending, challenging the effectiveness of traditional lead generation methods. Marketers were compelled to reassess their strategies for acquiring leads in this new economic reality. As a response to these challenges, the concept of lead magnets emerged as a pivotal development in the industry. Lead magnets are valuable incentives offered to potential customers in exchange for their contact information. They gained prominence because they offered a mutually beneficial solution: businesses could capture leads more effectively, while consumers received valuable resources. This shift in the approach to lead generation marked a crucial moment in the industry's evolution, emphasizing the importance of providing value and nurturing relationships with prospects in a more demanding economic environment

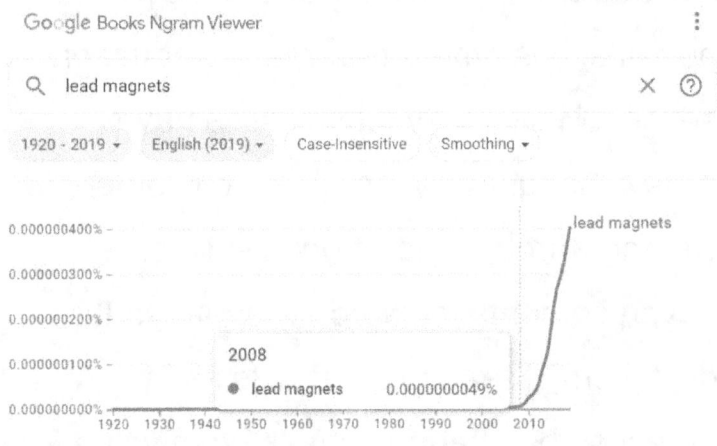

Lead Magnets

The term 'lead magnet' may be new, but most of the principles behind them are as old as time.

What are the principles?

Attraction: The idea here is to draw potential customers towards a product or service. Historically, businesses have always sought ways to attract customers, whether through storefront displays, advertisements, or word-of-mouth. In the digital era, a lead magnet acts as this attraction by offering something of value for free or at a minimal cost.

Exchange: This principle involves the notion of giving something to receive something in return. Traditionally, this might have been a sample product, a demonstration, or valuable information in exchange for a customer's attention or contact details. Something they can consume and/or experience that will greatly benefit their journey.

Limitless Ability for Strategic Generosity:
To ensure your advertisement comes out on top, simply adopt this principle. In today's cutthroat market, outshining your competitors means consistently offering more than expected to your audience. This approach revolves around strategic generosity, where you go the extra mile, leaving a memorable impression on potential customers. It's not merely about attracting leads; it's about consistently delivering exceptional value, nurturing trust, and forging enduring relationships. Embracing this principle urges businesses to adapt, innovate, and stay ahead in their industry, ultimately winning over leads abundantly and securing a distinctive competitive edge.

Building Relationships: Trust and relationship-building have always been at the core of business transactions. Lead magnets are a modern tool to initiate this process. By providing something valuable upfront, businesses start a relationship with potential customers, setting the stage for future interactions and sales.

Segmentation and Personalization: Understanding and catering to specific customer needs has been a long-standing practice in business. Lead magnets allow for segmentation (identifying different groups within your target audience) and personalization (tailoring content to meet the specific needs or interests of these groups), which are key for effective marketing and sales strategies.

Creating a Sense of Reciprocity: This principle is based on the idea that when someone receives something of value, they feel a sense of obligation to give something back. In the context of lead magnets, when potential customers receive valuable information or services, they may feel more inclined to engage further with the company.

Psychological Triggers: Lead magnets often leverage psychological triggers like curiosity, fear of missing out (FOMO), and the desire for instant gratification. By offering something that seems immediately beneficial or exclusive, lead magnets tap into these innate human tendencies, encouraging potential customers to act quickly to obtain the offered value.

Perceived Value and Scarcity:
Philosophically, the value of an object or service is not just in its intrinsic qualities but in its perceived rarity or exclusivity. Lead magnets often create a sense of scarcity, suggesting that the free resource is available only for a limited time or to a limited number of people, thereby increasing its perceived value.

Social Proof and Conformity: From a psychological perspective, individuals often look to others when making decisions. Lead magnets that showcase testimonials, user numbers, or endorsements tap into the principle of social proof, where potential customers are more likely to engage if they see others doing the same.

Commitment and Consistency: According to the principle of commitment and consistency in psychology, once a person commits to something small (like providing an email address), they are more likely to engage in further actions consistent with the initial commitment. This principle is often utilized in lead magnet strategies to nurture leads through a sales funnel.

Reciprocal Altruism: This concept from evolutionary psychology suggests that acts of giving and cooperation are beneficial for survival. In the context of lead magnets, when a business offers something valuable for free, it triggers a sense of reciprocal altruism, making the recipient more likely to reciprocate in some form.

Narrative Persuasion: Humans are wired to respond to stories, a concept deeply rooted in philosophy and psychology. Effective lead magnets often incorporate storytelling elements, creating a narrative around the product or service that resonates on an emotional level with potential customers.

Cognitive Dissonance: The theory of cognitive dissonance in psychology suggests that people have an inherent desire to maintain internal consistency. A well-crafted lead magnet can create a state of dissonance (e.g., between a person's current knowledge or situation and what the lead magnet offers), compelling the individual to resolve this dissonance by engaging further with the brand.

Existential Value and Self-Actualization: Drawing from existential philosophy and Maslow's hierarchy of needs, some lead magnets appeal to deeper desires for self-actualization and personal growth. They promise not just a tangible product or service, but also an opportunity for the individual to achieve a higher sense of purpose or fulfillment.

Hero's Journey: This concept, derived from Joseph Campbell's work in mythology, outlines a common pattern of adventure and transformation found in many stories worldwide. In the context of lead magnets, this can be employed by framing the customer's journey as a heroic narrative. The lead magnet becomes the 'call to adventure', offering the potential customer a path to overcome challenges or achieve goals. By positioning the product or service as an essential tool in this journey, the lead magnet resonates deeply with the customer's desire for transformation and accomplishment. The narrative of the customer's journey, with the lead magnet serving as a catalyst for their personal or professional transformation, taps into deep-rooted storytelling traditions and psychological desires for growth and achievement.

Superlatives Theory: This theory relates to the use of superlatives (e.g., most, best, fastest, easiest, highest) in marketing and communication. In psychology, superlatives can create a perception of superiority and desirability. When applied to lead magnets, using superlatives can enhance the perceived value and effectiveness of what is being offered. It appeals to the customer's desire for the best solutions, positioning the lead magnet as not just a beneficial choice, but the optimal one. By employing superlatives in the description and presentation of lead magnets, marketers can elevate the perceived value and uniqueness of their offerings, aligning with the psychological inclination towards choosing options that are presented as the best or most effective.

Value Proposition Clarity: In a world filled with information noise, clarity is your greatest ally. A compelling lead magnet not only captures attention but also succinctly communicates its value proposition. It's a promise, a solution, a glimpse of what awaits—an invitation to discover the transformation that lies within. When clarity reigns, curiosity follows, and potential customers find themselves drawn toward the beacon of your message.

Targeted Content: The power of a lead magnet lies in its precision. It's the art of speaking directly to the hearts and minds of those who seek what you offer. Targeted content resonates deeply, addressing the specific desires and dilemmas of your chosen audience. It's a magnetic force that says, "I understand you, and here's exactly what you need." In the world of lead magnets, relevance is the currency of connection.

Measurable Objectives: Lead magnets are not just offerings; they're milestones on your journey. To navigate the path of marketing success, you need clear signposts. Measurable objectives are those markers that guide your way, telling you whether you're on course or need a course correction. They're the data-driven compass that keeps you focused, adaptable, and always moving forward.

Multichannel Integration: In a world where your audience roams across digital landscapes, your lead magnet should be an omnipresent beacon. Multichannel integration is the art of extending your reach. It's about casting a wide net while maintaining a unified message. Your lead magnet should seamlessly traverse platforms, from social media scrolls to email inboxes, leaving a trail of engagement in its wake.

Feedback Loop: The wisdom of your audience is a precious gift. A feedback loop is the open channel through which you receive this gift and, in turn, refine your offerings. It's an invitation for your audience to guide your journey, to tell you what resonates and what needs improvement. In the world of lead magnets, it's a two-way street of understanding and growth.

Continuous Improvement: Stagnation has no place in the world of lead magnets. It's a dynamic landscape where evolution is the key to enduring success. Continuous improvement means a commitment to staying relevant, to adapting, to never settling for 'good enough.' It's the engine that propels you forward, ensuring that your lead magnets remain as vibrant and effective as the day they were conceived.

Compliance and Data Privacy: In a world of digital interactions, trust is the currency of exchange. Compliance with data privacy regulations is the bedrock of that trust. It's the assurance that you respect the sanctity of personal information, that you uphold ethical standards, and that you safeguard what has been entrusted to you. In the realm of lead magnets, compliance is the guardian of integrity.

Brand Consistency: Your brand is not just a logo or a name; it's an identity etched into the minds of your audience. Brand consistency in lead magnets reinforces that identity. It's the promise that what they see aligns with what they know. It's the thread that weaves a seamless narrative, ensuring that every encounter with your lead magnets is a chapter in the larger story of your brand.

Cross-Promotion: Strength lies in unity, and cross-promotion is the alliance of your marketing efforts. It's the art of amplifying your lead magnets' reach by tapping into existing resources. It's the recognition that your audience is interconnected, and by leveraging one lead magnet to shine a light on another, you create a web of engagement that stretches beyond individual offerings.

Resource Investment: Creating remarkable lead magnets is not just an endeavor; it's an investment in your audience's trust and engagement. It's an acknowledgment that quality resonates, that effort yields results, and that resources dedicated to crafting valuable lead magnets are resources wisely spent. It's the understanding that every investment paves the way for meaningful connections.

Responsive Design: In a digital world brimming with diverse devices, your lead magnets should adapt seamlessly to all screens. Responsive design is the bridge that connects you to your audience, regardless of the device they use. It's the assurance that your message will be crystal clear whether viewed on a desktop, tablet, or smartphone. In the realm of lead magnets, responsiveness is the key to accessibility.

Clear Exit Strategy: The journey doesn't end when a lead magnet is engaged; it's just the beginning. A clear exit strategy is the roadmap that guides your leads along the path of their journey with your brand. It's the plan for nurturing them, offering more value, and ultimately guiding them to the destination of conversion. In the world of lead magnets, clarity extends beyond attraction—it extends to the entire customer lifecycle.

Testing Frequency: Adaptation is the cornerstone of progress. In the realm of lead magnets, frequent testing is your laboratory for innovation. It's the laboratory where hypotheses are formed, experiments conducted, and insights harvested. It's the commitment to staying ahead of the curve by fine-tuning your lead magnets based on real-world results.

Arena: When your post/ad is displayed, each platform becomes an arena, and its users are the spectators in the stands. If they resonate with your content, these arenas come alive with excitement, possibly even erupting into a roar of approval, leading to your content going viral – much like the electrifying echo of a cheering crowd.

Managing Ad Campaigns: Managing ad campaigns involves building and nurturing your traffic sources. It's crucial not to overly rely on a single successful creative or platform; instead, diversify your approach. Continuously explore new avenues or consistently work on expanding your reach. Be content and format aware for each platform, ensuring that your messaging aligns seamlessly with the unique characteristics and preferences of your chosen channels. Additionally, be sure to check ad policies for each platform; you'll be surprised how unique they may be. Understanding and adhering to these policies is essential to maintaining successful and compliant ad campaigns.

200 Examples

Hopefully, this list will ignite your creativity and inspire you to develop the most effective, original and unique of lead magnets in your market. Have fun!

General examples:

1. Playbooks
2. Models
3. Workbooks
4. Roadmaps
5. Checklists
6. Previews
7. Guides, e-guides
8. Books, e-books
9. Audiobooks
10.   Recordings, replays

11. Webinars

12. Lookbook

13. Glossaries

14. Transcripts

15. Exploring pros and cons

16. Quizzes

17. Self assessments

18. Episodes

19. Behind-the-scenes

20. Visualizations

21. Infographics

22. Blueprints

23. Calendars

24. Trackers

25. Courses, mini-courses, micro-courses

26. Classes, masterclass

27. Masterminds

28. Lessons

29.   Lectures

30.   Teachings

31.   Highlights

32.   Best moments

33.   Crash courses

34.   Trainings

35.   Tutorials, instructions

36.   Widgets

37.   Browser extensions

38.   Trials

39.   System overviews

40.   Step-by-steps

41.   Workshops

42.   Workbooks

43.   Presentations

44.   Breakdowns

45.   Overviews

46.   Outlines

47.   Samples, samplers, testers

48.   Freebies

49.   Templates

50.   Access to community, group
   chats

51.   Earlybird access

52.   Whitepapers

53.   Case studies

54.   Research, reports

55.   Exclusive videos, series

56.   Cheatsheets

57.   Worksheets

58.   Hacks

59.   Go-arounds

60.   Toolkits

61.   Calculators

62.   Tools, softwares, apps

63.   Shortcuts

64.   Resources

65.   Links

66. Events, meetups, virtual events/meetups

67. Tickets, check-ins

68. Recipes

69. Research summaries

70. Lookbooks

71. Forms

72. Manuals

73. Skins

74. Flashcards

75. Presets

76. Collections

77. Lists

78. Memberships

79. Tips, tricks, collections etc

80. Frameworks

81. Strategies

82. Techniques

83. Stories

84. Printables

85. Demos

86. Exams

87. Audits

88. Reviews

89. Feedback

90. Mentorship

91. Coaching

92. Advice

93. Explainers

94. Comparison charts

95. Plans

96. Strategies

97. Frameworks

98. Action plans

99. Actionable steps, roadmaps

100. Maps, mind maps

101. Rules

102. Tips, tricks

103.   Top charts (top 5 xyz's)

104.   Principles, core principles, underlying principles

105.   Fundamentals, fundamental truths, fundamental principles

106.   First principle truths

107.   Tenets

108.   Ideas

109.   Reasons

110.   Formulas

111.   Wisdom-heavy quotes that resonate

112.   How to/is/did/do/does/will/would..

113.   Whats

114.   Whys

115.   Whens

116.   Wheres

117.   Noob vs Pro examples and
scenarios

118.   How-not-to, why-not-to, when-
not-to etc

119.   Discounts, coupons, promos,
codes, vouchers

120.   Consultations, discovery calls,
appointments,

121.   Estimates

122.   Quotes

123.   Assessments

124.   Evaluations

125.   Pre-qualifications

126.   Get started without xyz

127.   No credit card required

128.   Applications

129.   Interviews

130.   Infographics

131.   Podcasts

132. Tutorials

133. Demos

134. Slideshows

135. Audiobooks

136. Recipes

137. Strategies

138. Blueprints

139. Formulas

140. Insights

141. Analysis

142. Stories

143. Excerpts

144. Sneak Peeks

145. Bundles

146. Charts

147. Graphs

148. Data Sheets

149. Flashcards

150. Forums

170. Game Plans

171. Handbooks

172. Idea Banks

173. Interviews

174. Jokes

175. Keynotes

176. Laws

177. Manifestos

178. Newsletters

179. Opinions

180. Questionnaires

181. Scenarios

182. Tests

183. User Guides

184. Vlogs

185. Reflections

186. Surveys

187. Toolkits

188. Use Cases

189. Vouchers

190. Daily, Weekly, Monthly shows/series

191. Noteworthy Stuff

192. X-factors

193. Digests

194. Insights

195. Timelines

196. Scorecards

197. Decision Trees

198. Flowcharts

199. Idea Banks

200. Thought Leaders

201. Trend Reports

202. Pathways

203. Resolutions

204. Security, safety, safeguards

205. Protection, insurance

206.   Efficiency, productivity, time
    management

207.   Best Practices

Thank Yous

Thank you, Dad. Thank you, Mom.
Thank you to everybody who helped and
supported me in any way!

www.ingramcontent.com/pod-product-compliance
Lightning Source LLC
Chambersburg PA
CBHW062258290526
45794CB00006B/2610

* 9 7 9 8 8 6 3 5 8 3 6 1 7 *